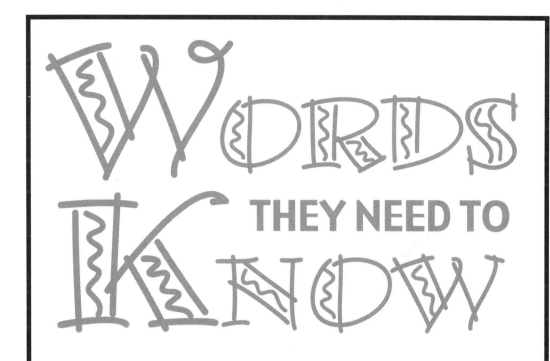

WORDS THEY NEED TO KNOW

A BOOK OF K-3 SIGHT WORD ACTIVITIES

by Sheron Brown & Sally Oppy

Teaching Resource Center

Published by
Teaching Resource Center
P.O. Box 82777, San Diego, CA 92138
1-800-833-3389
www.trcabc.com

Edited by Alice Handley
Design & production by Janis Poe

PRINTED IN THE UNITED STATES OF AMERICA ISBN: 1-56785-052-9

Contents

Introduction

Why Teach Sight Words?

Reading is all about constructing meaning from text. The meaning is derived from what readers bring to the text as well as what they discern from the text. That meaning is dependent on the rapid, automatic, and effortless recognition of words.

According to Patricia Cunningham in *Phonics They Use*, "In order to read and write fluently with comprehension and meaning, children must be able to automatically read and spell the most frequent words. As the store of words they can automatically read and spell increases, so will their speed and comprehension."

Readers need to recognize each word as quickly and effortlessly as possible so that they can pay attention to the more mentally demanding task of understanding what they are reading. "When children at an early age learn to recognize and automatically spell the most frequently occurring words, all their attention is freed for decoding and spelling less frequent words and more importantly, for processing meaning." (Cunningham, 2000)

Choosing the words on which to focus children's attention is a matter of efficiency. According to research there are words that appear more frequently than others in print. In fact:
- 13 words account for approximately 25% of all words in school texts (Johns, 1997): *a, and, for, he, in, is, it, of, that, the, to, was, you;*
- 109 words account for 50% of the words in school texts (Adams, 1990);
- the first 300 instant words make up about 65 percent of all written material (Fry, 1993).

These words are referred to as "sight words," "high frequency words," or "instant words."

The activities suggested help your students learn these sight words and tap into a wide range of learning modalities, including visual, auditory, kinesthetic, and visual-motor.

Why These Particular Sight Words?

The sight words selected for instruction in this book are the first 300 words of the American Heritage List of 1,000 most frequently used words in the English written language. Students will encounter these words more frequently than any other words in print and, for this reason, they need to recognize them on sight, and need to read them without hesitation.

How Is This Book Organized?

The book is organized into 3 sections: Assessment, Activities, and Blackline Masters.

Assessment should inform instruction; therefore, the first section explains the assessment of student sight word knowledge. The necessary blacklines for the assessment sheets follow.

The second section details the many activities included to help increase your students' sight word knowledge. These activities focus on a select number of sight words, garnered from your assessment of the student's needs. These activities are consistent in structure, so that your students can focus on the content of the learning, rather than on the mechanics of the activity.

The sight word activities are broken into three subsections: Word Card Activities, Magnetic Letter Activities, and Writing Activities. All the directions and materials needed are listed in this section.

The third section contains the necessary learning center cards, gameboards and word cards needed for the activities. Record-keeping forms are also included for two purposes: to make management of your students' word study activities efficient and to inform your word study instruction throughout the year.

How Do I Fit Sight Word Activities Into My Instructional Day?

The sight word activities included in this book are designed for the independent practice time of your language (literacy) block. These word activities may be placed at a literacy center. Some could certainly be in a student's own workspace, while others could be conducted with an adult (teacher, volunteer, aide, assistant). They are designed for individual, partner, or small group settings.

Prior to the students' independent practice of their words, the teacher should model and demonstrate the assigned sight word activity. The activities in this book are designed to enable your students to practice these words as a part of your classroom's overall word study instruction. For further reading on how word study and sight word instruction fit into a literacy block structure, refer to *Classrooms that Work, Phonics They Use, Words Their Way,* and *Word Matters,* available through TRC.

How Do I Manage Sight Word Activities?

Teaching students to operate in the independent sight word activity centers is crucial to having students be successful at any type of independent activity. Taking instructional time to train students in the each one of the independent sight word activities given in this book is instructional time well spent.

While the activities may change, the students need to operate in a consistent manner within each center. Students need to complete a given sight word activity by following a consistent procedure in a consistent location.

For example, if student partners are going to complete the Make It, Say It activity, they would pick up their individual file folders and a file folder for the Make It, Say It activity. Student partners would know where to complete the Make It, Say It activity, which would stay the same over time. They would know what voice level to use, how to solve challenges they experience, and at what point in time to begin returning materials to the correct locations. In other words, they would have all the knowledge and training necessary in order to operate independently, no matter which sight word activity they have been assigned.

How Do I Manage Sight Word Materials?

In a student-accessible location, keep a file folder for each student with his name clearly visible.

In each student's folder, maintain:
- the student's current set of 25 word cards, held in a plastic resealable bag, with the student's name written on the bag in permanent ink
- current assessment record keeping sheet, stapled to the inside front cover of the file folder. Additional assessment record keeping sheets may be stapled on top of each other as the child masters each list of sight words
- learning center card(s) for the sight word activity(ies) the student has been assigned for the selected time period

In a student-accessible location, keep a file folder for each activity with multiple sets of the appropriate materials for each sight word activity.

There are several effective partnering strategies that may be used. In a classroom setting where the goal is to have partners working independently, it is crucial that the partners be equal in their sight word knowledge, as much as possible. This assures that the partners are able to check each other's work accurately. Another possibility is the use of cross-age tutors or parent volunteers to ensure accurate checking of sight word activities.

How Do I Assess My Students for Sight Word Knowledge?

Benefits of Sight Word Assessment

- Provides an instructional starting point for the teacher
- Enables the teacher to focus sight word instruction where it is needed
- Enables the teacher to have knowledge of students' on-going progress as they learn their high frequency words

Initial Sight Word Assessment

Materials Needed:
- Two copies of the same list of 25 sight words; one for the student to read and the other for the teacher to record word recognition errors. (see pages 34-39)

Recommended Assessments:
- Grade 1: Sight Word Lists 1-4
- Grade 2: Sight Word Lists 1-8
- Grade 3: Sight Word Lists 1-12

Procedure:
1. The setting is one-to-one. Often this will be the classroom teacher and the student, although it could be a trained paraprofessional or a classroom volunteer and the student.
2. The purpose of the assessment is to identify sight words unfamiliar to the student. You are looking to gather between five and fifteen words, with which the student will work, using the sight word activities found in this book.
3. Ask the student to read the words on the list to you, in the order they appear.
4. Make a mark to indicate an error (circle, mark through, or put a dot beside the word).
5. Each student's assessment should take between two and four minutes.
6. Once you have gathered between five and fifteen words, stop the assessment.
7. Consider a word on a word list unfamiliar if a student does not instantly recognize the word, attempts to sound it out, or miscalls the word and then correctly identifies it.
8. The goal of the activities in this book is instant and automatic recognition of each sight word.

Ongoing Sight Word Assessment

Each student will need to have new words to work with as she masters the words you gathered during the initial assessment.

Procedure:
1. After a student has had multiple opportunities to work with her words using the many sight word activities in this book, reassess the student by using her original sight word list.
2. If the student reads the list words correctly and without hesitation, she will need a new set of words. You may consult the previous assessment in order to select the next five "unknown" words or you may move to the next higher list of sight words. Record-keeping sheets, found on pages 40-51, will make this process very efficient.
3. Any words read incorrectly during an assessment process should be included in the student's next set of five sight words.
4. Continue this process: reassessing the student as she masters sight words and thereby finding new words for her to master. Keep careful records using the record keeping sheets. As the student becomes more proficient at reading sight words, you will need to use the next higher lists to find new, unfamiliar words to challenge her.
5. Ongoing assessment will support your students' progress in adding to their sight word vocabularies at their own learning paces.
6. These ongoing assessments will take as little as a few seconds to no longer than two minutes per student to administer.

The following are the teacher directions for all activities.

Word Card Activities

SIGHT WORD DRAW

Setting   A partner or small group activity for students who are working within the same sight word list

Materials
- Word cards from the sight word list
- Draw 2 Card(s)
- Learning center card, page 19

Procedure
1. Students play Sight Word Draw using word cards. They choose the set of 25 from which they are working.
2. Word cards are placed face down on the center of the space and students take turns pulling one word card from the pile, or two cards if the Draw 2 card is chosen.
3. If he can read the word card, he puts it face up in front of himself. If he cannot identify the word, he returns the word card, face down, to the center pile and it is the next player's turn. The player with the most word cards at the end of the game, when all the cards have been drawn from the center pile, is the winner.
4. A student who has previously mastered the word list in play could be the "checker," to determine the correctness of the word cards read.

CARD RING/FAN PRACTICE

Setting   A partner activity for students who are working within the same Sight Word list

Materials
- Learning center card, page 20
- Word cards from the sight word list, laminated, with a hole punched in the left side, and threaded onto a metal O ring

Procedure
1. Students start by turning each word card on the ring and saying the words softly to themselves.
2. After the students have independently practiced their card rings, they alternate showing each other one card at a time from their ring and having the partner call out the word.
3. Partners can repeat this procedure of independent study and partner practice two to three times per activity session.

OPEN-ENDED GAMES

Setting   An activity for two to four students who are working within the same sight word list

Materials
- Word cards from the sight word list
- One die
- Colored game piece markers for each student.
- Open-ended game board(s) (pages 76-79). The boards are designed to be used individually or to be placed end-to-end to make a longer game and may be laminated or backed with a file folder
- Learning center card, page 21

Procedure
1. Each player chooses a game marker.
2. A set of word cards from a sight word list should be shuffled and placed face down on the game board area.
3. Players roll the die to determine the order of play. Each player in turn rolls the die, and chooses the card on the top of the stack. If he is able to read the word he can move his game piece forward the number of spaces that matches the number on the die.
4. If a player is unable to read the sight word card, she returns the card to the bottom of the stack.
5. The winner is the player who reaches the end of the game board first.
6. The game cards may be reshuffled and the game replayed.

CONCENTRATION

Setting   A partner activity for two students who are working within the same sight word list

Materials
- Two copies of the word cards from the sight word list
- Learning center card, page 22

Procedure
1. Shuffle the combined sets of sight word cards and lay the word cards face down in five rows of ten cards each. (If you think this is too many words, then only display half of the total cards at a time.)
2. A player turns over two word cards and reads them aloud. If the cards match and she has read them correctly, the cards are picked up and kept face up on her side. If the cards don't match, they are laid face down in their original position.
3. It is important that the cards remain in their original positions because this game relies on visual memory.
4. When all word cards have been matched, the player with the most pairs of cards on her side is the winner.
5. The game cards may be reshuffled and the game replayed.

POINT, SAY, AND TOUCH

Setting   A partner activity for students who are working within the same sight word list

Materials   • The five word cards each student is currently focusing on along with three other word cards from the same sight word list
   • Learning center card, page 23

Procedure
1. Partner One lays down all eight word cards face up.
2. Partner Two looks at the word cards and says to Partner One, "Show me _____(word)."
3. Partner One looks at the word cards and actually touches the word card and says it softly to Partner Two.
4. Partner Two then repeats the same "Show me _____" procedure with another word card.
5. When Partner One has touched and said each word three times, he picks up his word cards and Partner Two lays her word cards down face up.
6. Partner One then becomes the "Show me _____ (word)" student while Partner Two touches and says the requested words.
7. If, during the Point, Say, and Touch process an incorrect word card is "touched," the "Show me Partner" simply touches the correct word card, and then asks for the word to be touched again.

TIC-TAC-TOE

Setting   An activity for two students who are working within the same sight word list

Materials   • Blackline master of Tic-Tac-Toe board, page 82.
   • Word cards from the sight word list
   • 5 X cards and 5 O cards, page 82.
   • Learning center card, page 24

Procedure
1. Partner One chooses nine of his word cards and places them on the Tic-Tac-Toe board.
2. Partners take turns choosing a word card to read aloud to their partner. If one reads the card correctly, he puts an X or O on top of the word card read correctly.
3. The partner who gets Tic-Tac-Toe first is the winner.
4. Partner Two may then choose nine word cards to place on the Tic-Tac-Toe board and the game may be replayed, following the same procedure.

SIGHT WORD BINGO

Setting   An activity for four students who are working within the same sight word list

Materials
- Three copies of the blackline master of the Bingo board, page 80-81.
- List of sight words assigned to the students for the Caller
- Pencil/Eraser for Caller
- One package of colored game markers to cover word cards
- Word cards from the sight word list
- Learning center card, page 25

Procedure
1. Three players place 24 of their sight word cards on their Bingo card, in any order.
2. The Caller uses the sight word list and calls one word at a time.
3. Players place a colored game marker on top of the sight word and the Caller marks the word called on his list.
4. The game proceeds until one player has declared Bingo.
5. The winner reads the words from his card that earned the Bingo.
6. The Caller checks to be sure the words are read correctly.
7. The Caller erases the checks beside the words called and the winner becomes the new Caller.
8. The game may be replayed as time permits.

MATCHING ACTIVITIES

Setting   A partner activity for students working within the same sight word list

Materials
- Word cards from the sight word list (if desired, word cards from lists previously learned)
- category cards
- Learning center card, page 26

Procedure
1. Students place the word cards face up, in five rows of five cards each.
2. Students work cooperatively to organize the word cards by the category card.
3. Each student in turn picks up a word card, reads the word out loud and determines if it matches his category card.
4. If the word does not fit the category cards, it should be placed in the Discard stack.
5. Categories:
   - Match word cards that begin with the same letter.
   - Match word cards that end with the same letter.
   - Match word cards that begin with the same syllable.
   - Match word cards that end with the same syllable.
   - Match rhyming cards. (Most applicable with more than one set of sight word list cards.)
   - Organize cards alphabetically.
6. The teacher to reinforce phonics concepts being studied by the students may create additional category cards.

Magnetic Letter Activities

BENEFITS OF MAGNETIC LETTER ACTIVITIES

- Magnetic letter activities enable your students to practice their sight word recognition skills in a tactile way.
- Magnetic letters are colorful and appealing to students and provide a unique format for word practice activities.
- Magnetic letters are easy to handle for young children and develop eye/hand coordination.
- Magnetic letters remain in position so that a child can capture the visual picture of the sight word.
- Magnetic letters are non-consumable. Once the initial cost has been paid, they last a long time.
- For students in the First Grade, we highly recommend the magnetic letters that correspond to standard letter shapes. They give students added support in becoming sure of the letter shapes. As students become more confident of the letters and their shapes, the magnetic letter tiles are suitable.

MAKE IT, SAY IT

Setting   An individual or partner activity for students working within the same sight word list

Materials
- Magnetic letters in a divided box, sorted for letter retrieval
- Magnetic dry-erase board (9" x 12" is recommended)
- Word cards from the sight word list (It is recommended that students focus on the five words with which they are currently working. Additional words from the sight word list, which they have already mastered, could also be practiced.)
- Learning center card, page 27

Procedure
Individual Activity
1. The student looks at the word card and says the word in a soft voice.
2. Using the magnetic letters, the student makes the word on the board.
3. The student says the word aloud in a soft voice. He moves on to the second word card.
4. The student can repeat this procedure multiple times, according to teacher direction.

Partner Activity
1. Partner One shows a word card to Partner Two and asks her to make _____(word).
2. Using the magnetic letters, she makes the word on the board and then says the word aloud.
3. The partners move on to the second word card and follow the same procedure.
4. Partners may take turns either after each word, or after each partner has completed a set of five words.

MAKE IT, MIX IT, MAKE IT AGAIN

Setting   An individual or partner activity for students working within the same sight word list

Materials   • Magnetic letters in a divided box, sorted for letter retrieval
                • Magnetic dry-erase board (9" x 12" is recommended)
                • Word cards from the sight word list (It is recommended that students focus on the five words with which they are currently working. Additional words from the sight word list, which they have already mastered, could also be practiced.)
                • Learning center card, page 28

Procedure
Individual Activity
1. The student looks at the first word card.
2. Using the magnetic letters, the student makes the word on the board. The student says the word softly.
3. The student mixes the letters on the magnetic board and remakes the word, as quickly as she can, saying the word softly.
4. For a third time, the student mixes the letters and remakes the word, as quickly as possible, and says the word softly.
5. She then moves on to the second word. The student can repeat this procedure multiple times, according to teacher direction.

Partner Activity
1. Partner One shows word card to Partner Two and asks her to make _____(word).
2. Partner Two looks at the first word card and says the word softly.
3. Using the magnetic letters, she makes the word on the board and then says the word softly again.
4. Partner One mixes the letters on the magnetic board and asks Partner Two to remake the word, as quickly as possible and to say the word aloud.
5. For a third time, Partner One mixes the letters on the magnetic board and asks Partner Two to remake the word, even more quickly than she did the second time and to say the word aloud.
6. The partners switch roles and follow the same procedure for each word card.

MAKE IT, SAY IT, WRITE IT

Setting   An individual or partner activity for students working within the same sight word list

Materials
- Magnetic letters in a divided box, sorted for letter retrieval
- Magnetic dry-erase board (9" x 12" is recommended)
- Word cards from the sight word list (It is recommended that students focus on the five words with which they are currently working. Additional words from the sight word list, which they have already mastered, could also be practiced.)
- Dry-erase marker or paper and pencil
- Learning center card, page 29

Procedure
Individual Activity
1. The student looks at the first word card and says the word softly.
2. Using the magnetic letters, the student makes the word on the board. The student says the word softly.
3. The student writes the word on the magnetic dry-erase board or on a piece of paper.
4. He then moves on to the second word. The student can repeat this procedure multiple times, according to teacher direction.

Partner Activity
1. Partner One shows the word card to Partner Two and asks her to make _____(word).
2. Partner Two looks at the first word card and says the word softly.
3. Using the magnetic letters, she makes the word on the board and then says the word softly again.
4. Partner Two writes the word on the magnetic dry erase board or on a piece of paper.
5. Partner One uses the word card to check accuracy.
6. The partners switch roles and follow the same procedure for each word card.

WORD ELEVATORS

Setting   An individual activity

Materials
- Magnetic letters in a divided box, sorted for letter retrieval
- Magnetic dry-erase board (9" x 12" is recommended)
- Word cards from the sight word list (It is recommended that students focus on the five words with which they are currently working. Additional words from the sight word list, which they have already mastered, could also be practiced.)
- Appropriate Rimes for Sight Word List (pages 64-75) currently assigned. Place this in the student folder for him to use a reference.
- Learning center card, page 30

Procedure
1. Student will choose five to ten sight words from his current list. For each word selected he needs to think of three additional words with common rimes. (A rime is a vowel and any consonants that follow it.) For example, using the word card *and* in List 1, some rimes would be *sand, land,* and *hand*.
2. Using magnetic letters, the student makes the first word on the magnetic board and says the word softly to himself
3. The student thinks of other words that have the same rime. The student can refer to his rimes for the sight word list in his folder.
4. He finds the magnetic letters that form these new onsets (an onset is the initial consonant or blend preceding the vowel) and places them vertically in a line beneath the initial word from the sight word list.
5. For example, if the student has the words *and* and *in* on his word cards, the dry-erase magnetic board would look like:

and		in
h		p
l		t
s		w
st		th

6. The student mimics the movement of an elevator going down by moving the riming ending to complete the new word he makes at each "floor."
7. The student says each word softly to herself while making the word at each "floor."
8. For additional practice, the student can move the word elevator back up to the top "floor" and write the new words she has made on the magnetic dry erase board or on paper.

Writing Activities

WORD HUNTS

Setting   An individual or partner activity for students working within the same sight word list

Materials   • Previously read books from independent reading or any environmental classroom print
• Paper and pencil
• Highlighter pen or tape
• Sight word list student is currently assigned
• Learning center card, page 31

Procedure
1. The student hunts for her assigned sight words, looking through previously read independent reading books as well as environmental print in the classroom. These books can be classroom library books, books read during guided reading, or content area texts. The important factor here is that this is NOT new reading material for the student and the book must have been already read at least once.
2. When the student finds the word, she writes the word and its surrounding phrase on the piece of paper. The student highlights the sight word. She also writes the source of the word phrase.
3. For example: "As soon as he was out of sight…, page 3, The Mitten"
4. If there are no page numbers, the book title will suffice.

WRITE-A-SHAPE

Setting   An individual activity

Materials
- A blackline copy of one of the shapes from pages 84-89 or any simple shape you choose to provide
- Sharpened colored pencils or thin marking pens
- Sight word list the student is currently assigned
- Learning center card, page 32

Procedure
1. The student, using his five sight words, writes the sight words in consecutive order following the outline of the selected shape. For example, if the five words are *at, with, can, will,* and *you're* the student's Write-a-Shape work might look like this:

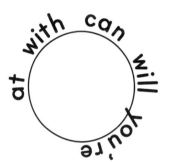

ABC WORD LIST SORT

Setting   An individual activity

Materials
- Word cards from the sight word list
- Paper and pencil
- Flat surface on which to sort word cards
- Alphabet picture cards, pages 90-91
- Learning center card, page 33

Procedure
1. The student sorts the word list cards under the alphabet picture card, categorizing words that begin with the same letter.
2. She takes these sets and alphabetizes them.
3. The student writes the letter that the words begin with at the top of a piece of paper. Under the letter she then writes all the words that begin with that letter.
4. Student says the beginning letter and the words on the list softly to herself.
5. The student may repeat the sort by mixing the cards and trying to do the activity more quickly the second time.

BLACKLINE MASTERS

SIGHT WORD DRAW

Setting   A partner or small group activity for students who are working within the same sight word list

What you will need
- Your word card set
- Draw 2 Card(s), cut from below

What you will do
1. Take the set of 25 word cards and the Draw 2 Card(s) and put them in the middle of the table, face down.
2. First, take the top card. Read it out loud and put it face up on your side.
3. If you cannot read the word, put it back on the pile face down.
4. If you select a Draw 2 card, take two cards from the stack.
5. Keep taking turns, until all the cards are gone.
6. The player with the most cards wins.

DRAW 2   DRAW 2

CARD RING/FAN PRACTICE

Setting   A partner activity for students who are working within the same sight word list

What you will need
- Two of the same card ring that you and your partner are working on

What you will do
1. Say each word on your ring softly to yourself.
2. Show the word cards to your partner one at a time and take turns saying the word to each other.
3. When you have finished, repeat the ring, saying the words to each other that you did not say the first time.

OPEN-ENDED GAMES

Setting   An activity for two to four students who are working within the same sight word list

What you will need
- Game board
- Game markers
- Your word card set
- One die

What you will do
1. Choose a game marker. Shuffle the word cards and put them in the middle of the game board, face down. Roll the die to see who goes first.
2. First, take the top card. Read it out loud and put it face up on your side. If you read the card correctly, move the game marker forward one space.
3. If you cannot read the word, put it back on the pile face down.
4. Keep taking turns, until all the cards are gone or until one of the players reaches the finish line.
5. The player who finishes first, or with the most cards when the stack is gone, wins.

CONCENTRATION

Setting   A partner activity for two students who are working within the same sight word list

What you will need
- Two sets of your word cards

What you will do
1. Shuffle the word card sets together and lay them face down on the table, in five rows of ten cards across.
2. Turn over two word cards and read them out loud. If you pick two that are the same and you read them correctly, you get to keep those two cards on your side, face up.
3. If the cards do not match, return them to their place, face down
4. Take turns until all the cards are matched.
5. The player with the most pairs of word cards on his side wins.

POINT, SAY AND TOUCH

Setting   A partner activity for students working within the same sight word list

What You Will Need
- Five of your word cards
- A flat work surface

What You Will Do
1. Lay your five word cards face up in front of you.
2. Your partner says, "Show me ____" and names one of the five word cards in front of you.
3. Look at the word cards, and touch the word card while repeating the requested word softly.
4. Your partner then repeats, "Show me___" and requests another word card.
5. Touch the word card while repeating the requested word softly.
6. When you have touched and said each word three times, pick up your word cards and have your partner lay his word cards down face up.
7. You then begin the "Show me____" requests while your partner does the touching and saying.

TIC-TAC-TOE

Setting   An activity for two students who are working within the same Sight Word list

What You Will Need
- Blackline master of Tic-Tac-Toe board
- Your word card set
- 5 X cards and 5 O cards

What You Will Do
1. Choose nine of your word cards and place them on the Tic-Tac-Toe board.
2. Take turns choosing a word card to read aloud to your partner. If you read the card correctly, put an X or O on top of that word card.
3. The partner who gets Tic-Tac-Toe first is the winner.
4. Now your partner may choose nine word cards to place on the Tic-Tac-Toe board. Play the game again.

SIGHT WORD BINGO

Setting   An activity for four students who are working within the same sight word list

What You Will Need

- Blackline master of a Bingo board for three players
- List of sight words assigned to the students for the Caller
- Pencil/Eraser for Caller
- One package of colored game markers to cover word cards
- A set of word cards from the sight word list

What You Will Do

1. Three players place 24 of their sight word cards on their Bingo card, in any order.
2. The Caller uses the sight word list and calls one word at a time.
3. Players place a colored game marker on top of the sight word and the Caller marks the word called on his list.
4. Continue until one player has declared Bingo.
5. The winner reads the words from his card that earned the Bingo.
6. The Caller checks to be sure the words are read correctly.
7. The Caller erases the checks beside the words called and the winner becomes the new Caller.
8. The game may be replayed as time permits.

MATCHING ACTIVITIES

Setting   A partner activity for students working within the same sight word list

What you will need

- Category cards
- Your word card set
- Set of sight word list cards from previous list (optional)

What you will do

1. Place category cards across the top of your work space.
2. Place the word cards face up in five rows of five cards each.
3. Work with your partner to read each of your words softly.
4. Decide together under which category each of the cards fits.
5. If a card does not fit into any category, place it under the Discard category.

After you have finished

Do it faster! Shuffle your cards and place them in the correct category again, saying the words softly.

MAKE IT, SAY IT

Setting   An individual or partner activity for students working within the same sight word list

What you will need
- A set of magnetic letters in a divided box
- A dry erase board
- Five or more of your word cards

What you will do
If you are by yourself
1. Look at your word card.
2. Make it with the magnetic letters.
3. Say the word in a soft voice.
4. Do this again with each word card.

If you have a partner
1. Show the word to your partner and ask him to make the word with the magnetic letters.
2. Ask your partner to say the word aloud softly to you.
3. Do this again with each word card.

MAKE IT, MIX IT, MAKE IT AGAIN

Setting   An individual or partner activity for students working within the same sight word list

What you will need

- A set of magnetic letters in a divided box
- A dry erase board
- Five or more of your word cards

What you will do
If you are by yourself

1. Look at your word card.
2. Make it with the magnetic letters.
3. Say the word aloud in a soft voice.
4. Mix the letters on the magnetic board and remake the word as quickly as possible.
5. Do this two more times with each word card.

If you have a partner

1. Show the word to your partner and ask him to make the word with the magnetic letters.
2. Ask your partner to say the word aloud softly to you.
3. Do this again with each word card.
4. Change partners twice more so that each partner makes the magnetic words three times.

MAKE IT, SAY IT, WRITE IT

Setting   An individual or partner activity for students working within the same sight word list

What you will need
- A set of magnetic letters in a divided box
- A dry erase board and marker or paper and pencil
- Five or more of your word cards

What you will do
1. Look at your word card.
2. Make it with the magnetic letters.
3. Say the word aloud in a soft voice.
4. Write the word on the white board or on your paper.
5. Do this again with each word card.

WORD ELEVATORS

Setting   An individual activity

What you will need
- Magnetic letters in a divided box
- Dry erase board and marker
- Your word card set

What you will do
1. Place the rhyming chunk after the first letter or letters that your teacher has written on your dry erase board.
2. Say the word softly to yourself.
3. Move the rhyming chunk down to each of the letters on your dry erase board, saying the new word softly to yourself.
4. You can practice moving the rhyming chunk up and down like an elevator, and say each word softly at each "floor."

After you have finished
Write each word elevator word on the dry erase board with a dry erase marker.

WORD HUNTS

Setting   An individual or partner activity for students working within the same sight word list

What you will need
- A set of books you have already read
- Paper and pencil
- Your list of sight words

What you will do
1. Look for the words on your list in any books you have already read or on any charts in your classroom.
2. When you find one of your words, write the list word you found and two or three words on either side of it on your paper. Also write the book's title and the page number where you found your word.
3. Continue looking for your list words in your books and around your room. Find as many of your words as you can.

WRITE-A-SHAPE

Setting   An individual activity

What you will need
- Five of your word cards
- A piece of paper with a shape outlined on it
- Colored pens or pencils

What you will do
1. Put your five word cards in front of you, in the order you wish to write them.
2. Pick the color or colors you wish to write your words in and write them along the lines of the shape.
3. Write the five words over and over again until you have written them, one after another, around the entire shape.

ABC WORD LIST SORT

Setting   An individual activity

What you will need
- Your word card set
- Paper and pencil
- Alphabet picture cards
- Desk or table

What you will do
1. Put all 25 word cards out in front of you.
2. Sort your word cards by beginning letter under the alphabet picture card.
3. If you have more than one card that begins with the same letter, look at the second or even third letter to put them into ABC order.
4. After you have sorted all of your word cards, write the words on your paper under their beginning letter.

After you have finished
Mix your word cards up again and see if you can put them in ABC order faster than you did the first time!

List One

the
of
and
a
to
in
is
you
that
it
he
for
was
on
are
as
with
his
they
at
be
this
from
I
have

List Two

or
by
one
had
not
but
what
all
were
when
we
there
can
an
your
which
their
said
if
do
will
each
about
how
up

List Three	List Four
out	its
them	who
then	now
she	people
many	my
some	made
so	over
these	did
would	down
other	only
into	way
has	find
more	use
her	may
two	water
like	long
him	little
see	very
time	after
could	words
no	called
make	just
than	where
first	most
been	know

List Five

get
through
back
much
before
go
good
new
write
out
used
me
man
too
any
day
same
right
look
think
also
around
another
came
come

List Six

work
three
word
must
because
does
part
even
place
well
such
here
take
why
things
help
put
years
different
away
again
off
went
old
number

List Seven	List Eight
great	end
tell	along
men	while
say	might
small	next
every	sound
found	below
still	saw
between	something
name	thought
should	both
Mr.	few
home	those
big	always
give	looked
air	show
line	large
set	often
own	together
under	asked
read	house
last	don't
never	world
us	going
left	want

List Nine

school
important
until
form
food
keep
children
feet
land
side
without
boy
once
animals
life
enough
took
sometimes
four
head
above
kind
began
almost
live

List Ten

page
got
earth
need
far
hand
high
year
mother
light
parts
country
father
let
night
following
picture
being
study
second
eyes
soon
times
story
boys

List Eleven	List Twelve
since	thing
white	whole
days	hear
ever	example
paper	heard
hard	several
near	change
sentence	answer
better	room
best	sea
across	against
during	top
today	turned
others	learn
however	point
sure	city
means	play
knew	toward
it's	five
try	using
told	himself
young	usually
miles	leave
sun	family
ways	song

Directions: Record a check mark by each word read correctly. If incorrectly read, record what the student said.

List One	Initial Assessment Date _____	Ongoing Assessment Date _____
the		
of		
and		
a		
to		
in		
is		
you		
that		
it		
he		
for		
was		
on		
are		
as		
with		
his		
they		
at		
be		
this		
from		
I		
have		

Directions: Record a check mark by each word read correctly. If incorrectly read, record what the student said.

List Two	Initial Assessment Date _____	Ongoing Assessment Date _____
or		
by		
one		
had		
not		
but		
what		
all		
were		
when		
we		
there		
can		
an		
your		
which		
their		
said		
if		
do		
will		
each		
about		
how		
up		

Directions: Record a check mark by each word read correctly. If incorrectly read, record what the student said.

List Three	Initial Assessment Date _____	Ongoing Assessment Date _____
out		
them		
then		
she		
many		
some		
so		
these		
would		
other		
into		
has		
more		
her		
two		
like		
him		
see		
time		
could		
no		
make		
than		
first		
been		

Directions: Record a check mark by each word read correctly. If incorrectly read, record what the student said.

List Four	Initial Assessment Date _____	Ongoing Assessment Date _____
its		
who		
now		
people		
my		
made		
over		
did		
down		
only		
way		
find		
use		
may		
water		
long		
little		
very		
after		
words		
called		
just		
where		
most		
know		

Directions: Record a check mark by each word read correctly. If incorrectly read, record what the student said.

List Five	Initial Assessment Date _____	Ongoing Assessment Date _____
get		
through		
back		
much		
before		
go		
good		
new		
write		
out		
used		
me		
man		
too		
any		
day		
same		
right		
look		
think		
also		
around		
another		
came		
come		

Directions: Record a check mark by each word read correctly. If incorrectly read, record what the student said.

List Six	Initial Assessment Date _____	Ongoing Assessment Date _____
work		
three		
word		
must		
because		
does		
part		
even		
place		
well		
such		
here		
take		
why		
things		
help		
put		
years		
different		
away		
again		
off		
went		
old		
number		

Directions: Record a check mark by each word read correctly. If incorrectly read, record what the student said.

List Seven	Initial Assessment Date _____	Ongoing Assessment Date _____
great		
tell		
men		
say		
small		
every		
found		
still		
between		
name		
should		
Mr.		
home		
big		
give		
air		
line		
set		
own		
under		
read		
last		
never		
us		
left		

Directions: Record a check mark by each word read correctly. If incorrectly read, record what the student said.

List Eight	Initial Assessment Date _____	Ongoing Assessment Date _____
end		
along		
while		
might		
next		
sound		
below		
saw		
something		
thought		
both		
few		
those		
always		
looked		
show		
large		
often		
together		
asked		
house		
don't		
world		
going		
want		

Directions: Record a check mark by each word read correctly. If incorrectly read, record what the student said.

List Nine	Initial Assessment Date _____	Ongoing Assessment Date _____
school		
important		
until		
form		
food		
keep		
children		
feet		
land		
side		
without		
boy		
once		
animals		
life		
enough		
took		
sometimes		
four		
head		
above		
kind		
began		
almost		
live		

Directions: Record a check mark by each word read correctly. If incorrectly read, record what the student said.

List Ten	Initial Assessment Date _____	Ongoing Assessment Date _____
page		
got		
earth		
need		
far		
hand		
high		
year		
mother		
light		
parts		
country		
father		
let		
night		
following		
picture		
being		
study		
second		
eyes		
soon		
times		
story		
boys		

Directions: Record a check mark by each word read correctly. If incorrectly read, record what the student said.

List Eleven	Initial Assessment Date _____	Ongoing Assessment Date _____
since		
white		
days		
ever		
paper		
hard		
near		
sentence		
better		
best		
across		
during		
today		
others		
however		
sure		
means		
knew		
it's		
try		
told		
young		
miles		
sun		
ways		

Directions: Record a check mark by each word read correctly. If incorrectly read, record what the student said.

List Twelve	Initial Assessment Date _____	Ongoing Assessment Date _____
thing		
whole		
hear		
example		
heard		
several		
change		
answer		
room		
sea		
against		
top		
turned		
learn		
point		
city		
play		
toward		
five		
using		
himself		
usually		
leave		
family		
song		

the	it	they
of	he	at
and	for	be
a	was	this
to	on	from
in	are	I
is	as	have
you	with	
that	his	

or	when	if
2	2	2
by	we	do
2	2	2
one	there	will
2	2	2
had	can	each
2	2	2
not	an	about
2	2	2
but	your	how
2	2	2
what	which	up
2	2	2
all	their	
2	2	
were	said	
2	2	

out	other	time
them	into	could
then	has	no
she	more	make
many	her	than
some	two	first
so	like	been
these	him	
would	see	

its	only	after
who	way	words
now	find	called
people	use	just
my	may	where
made	water	most
over	long	know
did	little	
down	very	

get	out	look
through	used	think
back	me	also
much	man	around
before	too	another
go	any	came
good	day	come
new	same	
write	right	

work	well	different
three	such	away
word	here	again
must	take	off
because	why	went
does	things	old
part	help	number
even	put	
place	years	

great	name	own
tell	should	under
men	Mr.	read
say	home	last
small	big	never
every	give	us
found	air	left
still	line	
between	set	

end	thought	together
along	both	asked
while	few	house
might	those	don't
next	always	world
sound	looked	going
below	show	want
saw	large	
something	often	

school	side	four
9	9	9
important	without	head
9	9	9
until	boy	above
9	9	9
form	once	kind
9	9	9
food	animals	began
9	9	9
keep	life	almost
9	9	9
children	enough	live
9	9	9
feet	took	
9	9	
land	sometimes	
9	9	

page	light	study
got	parts	second
earth	country	eyes
need	father	soon
far	let	times
hand	night	story
high	following	boys
year	picture	
mother	being	

since	best	it's
	11	11
white	across	try
	11	11
days	during	told
	11	11
ever	today	young
	11	11
paper	others	miles
	11	11
hard	however	sun
	11	11
near	sure	ways
	11	11
sentence	means	
	11	11
better	knew	
	11	11

thing	sea	five
12	12	12
whole	against	using
12	12	12
hear	top	himself
12	12	12
example	turned	usually
12	12	12
heard	learn	leave
12	12	12
several	point	family
12	12	12
change	city	song
12	12	12
answer	play	
12	12	
room	toward	
12	12	

the								
of								
and	band	bland	brand	hand	land	sand	stand	strand
a								
to	do	into	who					
in	bin	chin	fin	grin	pin	skin	spin	thin	win
is	his	tis						
you								
that	at	bat	cat	chat	fat	flat	hat	mat	pat
it	bit	fit	hit	kit	quit	pit	sit	spit	wit
he	be	me	she	we				
for	or							
was								
on	con	Don	Ron					
are								
as	has							
with	fifth	pith	Smith					
his	is	'tis						
they	hey	grey	prey					
at	bat	cat	chat	fat	flat	hat	rat	that
be	he	me	she	we				
this	Chris	dis	sis					
from								
I								
have								

or	for							
by	cry	dry	fly	my	spy	try	why	wry
one	done	none						
had	bad	dad	glad	mad	pad	sad		
not	blot	dot	got	hot	pop	rot	shot	spot	tot
but	cut	hut	nut	rut	shut	strut	tut	
what								
all	ball	call	fall	mall	small	stall	tall	wall
were								
when	amen	Ben	hen	men	pen	ten	then	wren
we	be	he	me	she				
there	where							
can	an	ban	man	pan	ran	scan	tan	van
an	ban	began	can	man	ran	span	tan	than
your	pour							
which	rich							
their								
said								
if								
do	ado	into	to	two	who			
will	dill	drill	fill	ill	mill	pill	sill	thrill
each	beach	bleach	peach	preach	reach	teach		
about	clout	grout	out	scout	shout	spout	stout	trout
how	brow	chow	cow	now	plow	vow	wow	
up	cup	pup	sup					

out	about	bout	clout	grout	scout	shout	spout	trout
them	gem	hem	stem					
then	amen	Ben	hen	men	pen	ten	when	wren
she	be	he	me	we				
many	any							
some								
so	also	ago	go	no	pro			
these								
would	could	should						
other	another	brother	mother	smother				
into								
has								
more	adore	before	pore	score	shore	store		
her								
two	ado	do	into	to	who			
like	alike	bike	hike	Mike	pike	spike	strike	
him	brim	dim	grim	prim	rim	slim	swim	trim
see	agree	bee	degree	flee	free	knee	tree	three
time	chime	crime	dime	grime	lime	mime	prime	slime
could	should	would						
no	ago	also	go	pro	so			
make	awake	bake	fake	lake	shake	snake	take	wake
than	an	ban	can	man	ran	tan		
first	thirst							
been								

its	bits	fits	hits	quits	skits	slits	splits
who	ado	do	into	to	two		
now	allow	bow	chow	cow	how	plow	vow	wow
people							
my	by	cry	dry	fly	shy	sky	try
made	evade	fade	grade	parade	shade	trade	wade
over	clover	rover					
did	hid	kid	lid	rid	skid	slid	squid
down	brown	clown	crown	frown	gown	town	
only							
way	bay	day	may	pay	play	say	stay	tray
find	behind	blind	grind	kind	mind	rind	unwind	wind
use	abuse	amuse	fuse	muse	refuse		
may	day	pay	play	say	stay	stray	tray	way
water							
long	along	belong	gong	prong	song	strong	wrong
little	belittle	spittle	whittle				
very							
after	rafter						
words							
call	all	ball	hall	mall	small	stall	tall	wall
just	bust	crust	dust	must	robust	rust	trust	unjust
where	there						
most	ghost	host	post				
know	aglow	below	bow	blow	low	row	show	snow

get	bet	fret	met	net	pet	set	wet	yet
through								
back	black	crack	Jack	quack	sack	shack	track	whack
much	such							
before								
go	ago	also	no	pro	so			
good	hood	stood	wood					
new	anew	blew	chew	crew	dew	drew	few	knew
write	bite	invite	kite	polite	recite	quite	site	white
out	about	bout	clout	grout	scout	shout	spout	trout
use	abuse	amuse	fuse	muse	refuse			
me	be	he	she	we				
man	an	can	fan	pan	plan	ran	than	van
too	boo	coo	goo	moo	shampoo	shoo	zoo	
any	many							
day	bay	may	pay	play	say	stay	tray	way
same	became	blame	came	frame	flame	game	name	tame
right	alright	bright	flight	fright	light	night	sight	tight
look	book	brook	cook	hook	nook	rook	shook	took
think	blink	drink	ink	link	pink	sink	slink	stink
also								
around	bound	ground	hound	pound	round	sound		
another	brother	mother	other	smother				
came	became	blame	frame	flame	game	name	same	tame
come	become	some						

work							
three	agree	bee	degree	free	knee	see	spree	tree
word							
must	bust	crust	dust	just	must	rust	trust	unjust
because							
does							
part	art	cart	chart	dart	depart	mart	smart	start
even							
place	brace	face	grace	lace	race	pace	space	trace
well	bell	cell	fell	sell	shell	smell	tell	yell
such	much						
here							
take	bake	cake	fake	lake	make	quake	shake	snake
why	by	cry	dry	fly	my	spy	try	wry
thing	bring	cling	king	ring	sing	spring	sting	wing
help	kelp	whelp	yelp				
put							
year	clear	dear	ear	fear	gear	hear	near	tear
different							
away							
again							
off	doff	scoff					
went	bent	cent	lent	rent	sent	scent	spent	tent
old	cold	fold	gold	hold	mold	scold	sold	told
number	lumber	slumber					

great

tell	bell	dell	fell	sell	shell	smell	spell	tell	well
men	amen	Ben	hen	pen	ten	then	when	wren	
say	day	clay	may	play	way				
small	ball	call	hall	mall	stall	stay	stray	tall	wall

every

| **found** | ground | hound | pound | round | sound | | | | |
| **still** | dill | drill | fill | ill | mill | pill | sill | skill | will |

between

| **name** | blame | came | frame | fame | flame | game | same | tame | |
| **should** | could | would | | | | | | | |

Mr.

home	dome	Rome	tome						
big	brig	dig	fig	jig	pig	rig	twig	wig	
give	forgive	live	relive						
air	chair	fair	hair	pair	repair	stair			
line	decline	fine	nine	pine	shine	spine	whine	wine	
set	bet	fret	get	met	net	pet	wet	yet	
own	blown	flown	grown	known	shown	thrown	unknown		
under	asunder	blunder	thunder						
read	bead	lead							
last	blast	cast	contrast	fast	mast	past	vast		
never	clever	ever	forever	however	lever	sever			
us	bus	plus	pus	thus					
left	bereft	cleft	deft	theft					

end	attend	bend	blend	lend	mend	send	spend	trend
along							
while	awhile	file	mile	Nile	pile	smile	tile
might	bright	flight	light	night	right	sight	tight	tonight
next	text						
sound	bound	found	ground	hound	pound	round	wound
below							
saw	claw	draw	jaw	law	paw	raw	straw
something							
thought	bought	brought	fought	sought			
both							
few	anew	blew	chew	crew	dew	knew	new	screw
those	chose	compose	expose	hose	nose	oppose	pose	rose
always	hallways						
look	book	brook	cook	hook	shook	took	
show	aglow	below	blow	glow	know	low	row	snow
large	barge	charge	discharge	enlarge			
often	soften						
together	feather	heather	weather	whether			
ask	bask	cask	flask	mask	task		
house	blouse	douse	louse	mouse	spouse		
don't	won't						
world							
going							
want							

school	cool	drool	fool	pool	stool	tool	
important							
until							
form	dorm	inform	norm	perform	reform	storm	
food	brood	mood					
keep	beep	creep	deep	jeep	sheep	sleep	sweep
children							
feet	fleet	greet	meet	sheet	street	sweet	tweet
land	band	brand	demand	expand	hand	sand	stand
side	bride	glide	hide	ride	slide	tide	wide
without							
boy	annoy	destroy	employ	enjoy	joy	soy	toy
once							
animals							
life	fife	knife	rife	strife	wife		
enough	rough	slough	tough				
took	book	brook	cook	hook	look	shook	
sometimes							
four	pour	your					
head	dead	lead	read				
above	dove	glove	love	shove			
kind	behind	blind	find	grind	mind	remind	wind
began							
almost							
live	forgive	give					

page	cage	engage	gage	sage	wage			
got	cannot	cot	dot	got	hot	lot	not	spot	tot
earth	dearth							
need	bleed	breed	feed	greed	seed	speed	steed	weed
far	car	bar	jar	scar	star	tar		
hand	band	brand	demand	expand	gland	land	sand	stand
high	nigh	sigh	thigh					
year	clear	dear	ear	fear	hear	near	tear	
mother	brother	other						
light	bright	flight	might	night	right	sight	tight	
part	art	cart	chart	smart	start			
country								
father								
let	bet	fret	get	met	net	pet	set	wet	yet
night	alright	bright	flight	light	might	right	sight	tight
following								
picture								
being								
study								
second								
eyes								
soon	balloon	croon	monsoon	moon	platoon	spoon	swoon	
time	dime	chime	crime	grime	lime	mime	prime	slime
story	glory	gory						
boy	annoy	decoy	destroy	employ	enjoy	joy	soy	toy	Troy

since	convince	prince	quince	wince			
white	bite	ignite	invite	kite	quite	site	write
day	bay	clay	hay	gray	may	play	say	way
ever	clever	forever	however	lever	never	sever	whatever
paper	caper	scraper	taper				
hard	bard	card	charred	guard	lard	scarred	yard
near	clear	dear	ear	fear	hear	tear	year
sentence							
better	fetter	letter	setter	wetter			
best	arrest	contest	digest	nest	rest	test	west
across							
during							
today							
others	brothers	mothers					
however							
sure	cure	endure	lure	mature	pure	secure	
mean	bean	clean	dean	jean	lean		
knew	anew	blew	chew	crew	drew	few	new
it's							
try	by	cry	dry	fly	my	shy	sky
told	cold	fold	gold	hold	mold	old	scold	sold
young							
mile	awhile	file	Nile	pile	smile	tile	while
sun	begun	bun	fun	gun	pun	run	spun
way	day	may	pay	play	say	stay	tray

thing	bring	cling	king	ring	sing	spring	sting	wing
whole	console	dole	mole	parole	pole	role	stole	
hear	appear	clear	dear	ear	fear	near	tear	year
example								
heard								
several								
change	derange	exchange	grange	range	strange			
answer								
room	boom	bloom	broom	doom	gloom	groom	loom	zoom
sea	flea	pea	tea					
against								
top	chop	cop	crop	drop	hop	mop	pop	shop	stop
turned								
learn	earn	yearn						
point	anoint	joint						
city	pity							
play	bay	day	hay	may	pay	say	stay	tray	way
toward								
five	arrive	dive	drive	hive	jive	live	strive	thrive
using								
himself								
usually								
leave	cleave	heave	weave					
family								
song	along	belong	gong	long	prong	strong	throng	wrong

Open Ended Game Board

Copy and tape the Bingo board together in the middle.

You need five words across, down or diagonal (corner to corner) to have a Bingo.

Tic-Tac-Toe

X X X X X

O O O O O

Cards that begin with
the same letter

Cards that
do not match

Cards that
do not match

Cards that
rhyme

Cards that end with
the same letter

Cards that
do not rhyme

Cards that
do not match

Cards in
ABC order

Cards that begin with
the same syllable

Discard

Cards that
do not match

Cards that end with
the same syllable

Write-a-Shape

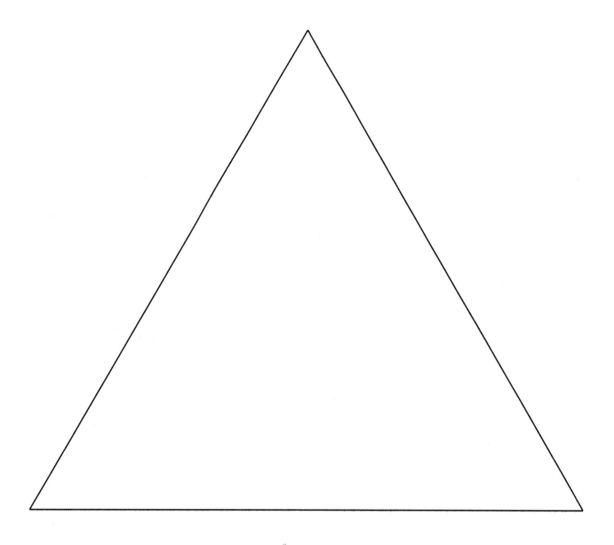

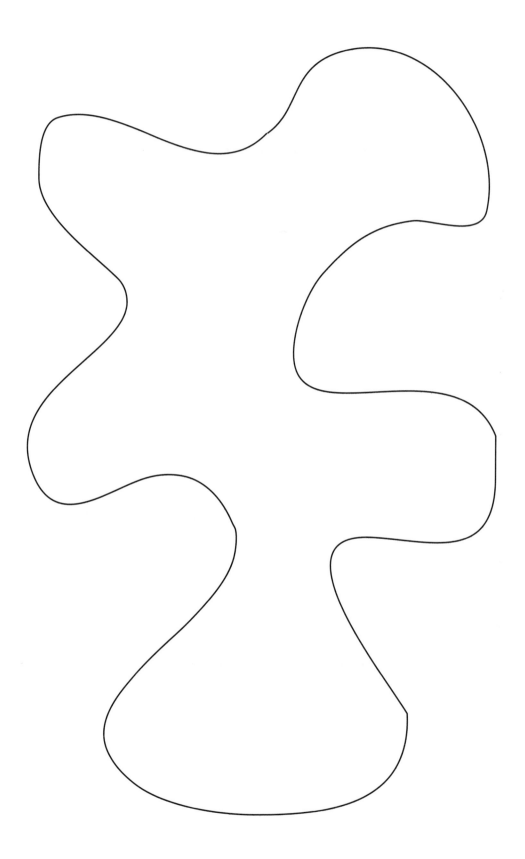

Professional References

Adams, Marilyn. *Beginning to Read: Thinking and Learning about Print.* Cambridge, MA, MIT Press, 1990.

Bear, Donald , Shane Templeton, Marcia Invernizzi and Francine Johnston. *Words Their Way.* Merrill/Prentice Hall, NJ, 1998.

Cunningham, Patricia and Richard Allington. *Classrooms That Work.* Harper Collins College Publishers, New York, 1994.

Cunningham, Patricia. *Phonics They Use.* Addison Wesley Longman, New York, 2000.

Fountas, Irene C. and Gay Su Pinnell. *Guided Reading.* Heinemann, Portsmouth, NH, 1996.

Fry, Edward, et all. *The Reading Teacher's Book of Lists.* Prentice Hall, NJ, 1993.

Lenski, Susan and Jerry L. Johns, *Improving Reading,* Kendall Hunt Publishing, Dubuque, IA, 2001

Pinnell, Gay Su and Irene C. Fountas. *Word Matters.* Heinemann, NH, 1998.